Original title:
It's Fine, I'm Fine, Everything's Not Fine

Copyright © 2024 Creative Arts Management OÜ
All rights reserved.

Author: Clara Allen
ISBN HARDBACK: 978-9908-0-0462-4
ISBN PAPERBACK: 978-9908-0-0463-1

Fractured Harmony

In a world that spins with glee,
I dance like a chicken, carefree.
The tune is all out of whack,
But I'm not looking to turn back.

My smile's a mask, but who cares?
I juggle my worries like chairs.
While laughter bubbles up like cream,
Inside, I'm caught in a wild dream.

Veils of Solitude

Behind curtains of laughter, I hide,
In a closet of jokes piled high, my pride.
They see the sparkles, the funny lights,
While shadows dance in solitary nights.

I'll wear my bright socks with flair,
A jester's heart laid bare.
With every quip and every pun,
No one knows how much I run.

Whims of the Unraveled

I'm a lunatic on a roller skate,
Spinning tales that can't be straight.
With each wild twist, I take a bow,
But inside, chaos makes me cow.

The jokes I tell become my shield,
In this battlefield, laughter's my field.
A punchline drops like a heavy stone,
But here I am, all alone.

The Weight of Unsaid Words

I carry secrets like a clown's big shoes,
With every giggle comes the blues.
Words hover near the tip of my tongue,
But laughter's the anthem I've sung.

In a crowd, I'm a beacon of cheer,
Yet inside screams nobody hears.
Jokes are my armor, my strange disguise,
While the truth waits for dawn to rise.

Beneath the Picture-Perfect

Smiles plastered on with glue,
Colors bright and all askew.
While the backdrop shines so bright,
Inside we're wrangling with the night.

Sprinkled laughter, confetti tears,
Whispers hiding all our fears.
Filters mask the daily grind,
In this frame, no peace we find.

Cracked Vessels

Teacups chipped, yet they hold tea,
Like our hearts, both cracked and free.
Pour a smile, let it spill,
Ignore the cracks, we've got the thrill.

With every toast, the glasses clink,
"Cheers" we shout, then stop to think.
What's beneath the porcelain sheen?
Kettle's boiling, we're not serene.

The Illusion of Safety

Cushioned corners, softened falls,
But inside rages, jumping walls.
Bubbles float, so bright and neat,
Yet pop they do in silent heat.

Hiding chaos in warm retreat,
Unruly thoughts that skip a beat.
Mask it all with painted cheer,
When the truth just won't stay clear.

Collapsing Facades

Walls made of laughter, paintpots bright,
Yet beneath, they crumble in the night.
Jokes are snippets, stitched with thread,
Inside we're just a bit misled.

Every faux pas held like gold,
But truths are whispers, shy and cold.
As layers peel, we start to see,
Behind the mask, who's really me?

Shattered Reflections

In the mirror, I grin wide,
Yet inside, there's quite a ride.
Jokes I tell, laughter floats high,
But shadows murmur, 'Oh, why try?'

My coffee spills, the cat takes a leap,
I laugh it off, but secrets creep.
The world spins round, what a funny race,
While chaos hides behind my face.

The Quiet Discontent

Wearing smiles like autumn leaves,
But under it, a heart deceives.
Whistling tunes of jolly cheer,
While doubts walk in, quite austere.

The dog barks loud, he makes a scene,
I chuckle, 'Life's a lovely dream!'
Yet underneath, a sneaky frown,
Like losing socks, I slip, fall down.

Veils of Illusion

A twinkling view from my window pane,
Yet storms are brewing, quite insane.
Laughing at woes, oh, what a trick,
Dancing in puddles, pick a stick.

With friends I jest, we joke, we play,
But inside whispers lead me astray.
A clownish mask, so bright and bold,
Hides a story that's rarely told.

A Heart in Dissent

I stroll through parks with a jaunty stride,
While in my chest, emotions bide.
Tickling thoughts and quirky dreams,
Conceal what's real, or so it seems.

Kites in the air, I wish to soar,
But the ground's got traps, I can't ignore.
Jokingly, I wave my hands,
Yet tangled truths form heavy strands.

Reflections on a Stormy Day

Raindrops dance on the windowpane,
Inside, I wear my best frown again.
The kettle screams, but I'm not awake,
Coffee? No, just my sanity's shake.

Dogs prance by in colorful coats,
While I dodge puddles with soggy notes.
A world so gray, yet I laugh at the mess,
Life's joke is bright in this dampness, I guess.

The thunder rumbles, what could it be?
Just my stomach, craving more tea.
Outside, the chaos, inside a grin,
Finding the joy where light should have been.

Umbrellas upside-down, fashion so bold,
I wear my quirks like stories untold.
Rain or shine, what's the difference to me?
Another fine day for absurdity!

Joy on the Brink

I trip on my own shoelaces, so neat,
Searching for joy in the crumbs at my feet.
Laughter erupts from a pasta mishap,
Life's little hiccups, I'm taking a nap.

The squirrel outside steals my muffin right quick,
He laughs as he scurries, what a cute little trick!
I wave my fist, but it's more of a dance,
This silly parade has given me a chance.

A cat flicks its tail, eyeing me sly,
As I stumble around, pretending to fly.
The mirror reflects my bewildered face,
What a circus this life, oh, what a race!

With each little blunder, I find a delight,
Joy's just a wink in the dim morning light.
I'll keep laughing loud, through chaos or calm,
For life's absurd mess is my favorite charm!

Beneath the Glossy Exterior

A smile painted on, so wide and bright,
While chaos dances just out of sight.
Lipstick on troubles, a charming disguise,
Who knew that laughter could hide such cries?

Coffee spills, but I sip with grace,
Chasing bliss in this frantic race.
Lip service states, 'I'm having a ball!'
Yet inside I'm tripping, about to fall.

Unseen Turmoil

Juggling life like a clown in a show,
With pies in the face, and stubbed toes below.
Calendar's packed, yet I'm lost in a haze,
Am I busy, or just in a daze?

In the crowd, I'm still all alone,
A king with no kingdom, just a rubber bone.
With rain clouds disguised as fluffy white fluff,
I laugh at the nonsense—it's silly, but tough.

The Dichotomy of Being

Confetti confusions, a party of strife,
All while pretending that's just how's life.
With outfits that sparkle and jokes that fall flat,
I wrestle my demons, how silly is that?

In a room full of jesters, I'm crowned as the fool,
Juggling my issues, like some crazy duel.
With balloons that pop, and laughter so loud,
I step on my dreams, and still feel so proud.

The Mirage of Normalcy

The grass looks perfect, but it's just a spray,
Underneath, it's a jungle gone wildly astray.
I text my best friend, 'It's all going great!'
But inside, I'm cringing— I just can't relate.

Dishes are stacked, like a tower of plates,
I laugh like a hyena, but please don't relate.
The romance of chaos feels beautifully sweet,
As I dance on the edge of a banana peel feat.

A Fragile Facade

I'm smiling like a fool,
While juggling my own thoughts.
The world's a playful game,
And I'm stuck in tie knots.

My coffee spills on time,
As I pretend to be chic.
I wear these fancy shoes,
But my balance feels weak.

Jokes tickle my strange heart,
In a circus of my mind.
I laugh at my own flaws,
While waving them, resigned.

So here's to life's grand act,
With a wink and a jest.
I dance through chaos here,
And pretend it's all the best.

Beneath the Surface

A duck floats on the pond,
Calm and cool in the breeze.
Underwater, it paddles,
With chaos meant to tease.

I smile at all my pals,
A mask that fits just right.
But beneath the surface lies,
A squawking, frantic fight.

A carefree laugh escapes,
While I tie my shoelace tight.
The world keeps spinning fast,
And I'm trapped in a light plight.

The duck quacks back at me,
A nod to my charade.
Together we both swim,
In this funny little parade.

The Calm Before the Storm

Clouds drift above my head,
As sunshine's lost its charm.
I pack my bags with hope,
Still wondering of the harm.

A cheerful breeze is here,
With caution in its tune.
The thunder laughs aloud,
As I balance on a spoon.

Smiles trade places wide,
With frowns across my face.
Like socks that don't quite match,
In life's chaotic race.

The calm is just a tease,
Preparing me for more.
Let's dance around the mess,
As life pulls out its score.

Flickers of Serenity

I light a candle bright,
In the corner of my room.
It flickers in the dark,
As worries start to bloom.

The cat is sprawled on books,
Like a fluffy little king.
While I juggle phone calls,
And pretend I can sing.

The calm within the storm,
Is a laugh wrapped in a sigh.
With every little blip,
I toss doubt in the sky.

So here's to chaos' grace,
And laughter in disguise.
For in each flicker found,
A calm surprise lies.

Masks of Serenity

With a smile painted bright,
I dance in the light,
Feigning joy in a crowd,
While chaos is loud.

Behind the laughter's charade,
A parade of charades,
Juggling woes with a grin,
While the inner me spins.

Sip my tea, murmur peace,
As my worries increase,
The calm in my gaze,
A cleverly crafted maze.

So I'll twirl through the day,
In this playful ballet,
When the world's in a twist,
Just try not to persist.

The Calm Beneath the Storm

Standing tall in the rain,
With a smirk, hide the pain,
Umbrella turned upside down,
I'm the jester, not the clown.

Raindrops laugh, fall and play,
On a light-hearted display,
My heart may be in shambles,
But oh, how my smile gambles.

Thunder rumbles with flair,
I flaunt confidence rare,
In the midst of the strife,
I choreograph my life.

Dance, oh woes, on my head,
While I sip lemonade red,
In this tempest's embrace,
Finding joy in the race.

Whispers of a Cracked Facade

Nodding as you speak,
While feeling so weak,
Words like bubbles they rise,
But pop with my sighs.

Behind my bright-eyed stare,
Lies a wonderland rare,
Cracks in the smile run deep,
Where secrets tend to creep.

Reality starts to slip,
As I balance, then whip,
For laughter's my disguise,
In a world full of lies.

I'll waltz on the edge,
In this whimsical pledge,
While you think it's all fine,
I dance to my own line.

Smiles in the Shadow

In the twilight I stand,
With a silly band,
Grinning bright like the sun,
While chaos quietly spun.

The moon winks just for fun,
As I juggle and run,
With the shadows in tow,
Feasting on fancy, a show.

Banana peels pave my path,
But I conjure a laugh,
As the missteps parade,
In this mischievous spade.

So here's to the jest,
In life's complicated quest,
Where smiles shield the fright,
And the shadows sing light.

Masks of Brass

With smiles so bright, we wear our charm,
Each chuckle hides a little harm.
The world spins round, a dizzy dance,
While we pretend to take our chance.

A jester's hat upon my head,
I juggle woes, then jump in bed.
The punchline's punch, it stings all night,
But laughter's glow, it feels so right.

We toast to life, a sparkling glass,
While secret frowns peek through the mask.
The raindrops Rhymed, our little joke,
We'll laugh and laugh, don't let it choke.

In shadows, whispers tickle deep,
Behind our masks, wild thoughts creep.
Each guffaw hides a little tear,
Yet here we are, let's raise a cheer!

Soliloquy of Strain

I prance about with anxious glee,
Inside my mind, a frantic spree.
The stars align, or so they say,
But here I sit, a twisted play.

My coffee cup's a throne divine,
With every sip, I sip the wine.
"Are you okay?" a friend might ask,
I grin and hide behind my mask.

The clock strikes three, my hair's a fright,
Yet here I stand, a comic sight.
Playing parts in this grand charade,
Where normalcy has slowly swayed.

Giggles echo in my head,
While worries dance just like the dead.
I'll juggle life, a circus show,
And laugh at all the undertow.

Dark Corners of Joy

In every corner, glimmers hide,
With funky struts, I take my stride.
A ticklish grin, a secret wave,
Joy wanders where the heart is brave.

Yet shadows lurk behind the cheer,
A soft reminder, 'You're not clear.'
I waltz with whirls of mock disdain,
Dance in the rain, ignore the pain.

When life throws pies of silly dreams,
I catch them with my frantic schemes.
A belly laugh is all I need,
To plant the funny, grow the seed.

So here I am, a jester wise,
With twinkling hopes that never die.
In darkened nooks, I find the light,
A wiggly dance, it feels so right.

The Facade Fades

I flip my hair, strike a pose of cool,
While inside, I'm just a cluttered fool.
With every smile, there's a twist of fate,
In this grand play, we contemplate.

A tiny laugh escapes my lips,
While chaos tugs at all my quips.
I tell a joke, it flops again,
But here's a laugh, I'll try, amen.

The curtains rise, the stage is set,
I wear a grin, no room for regret.
A twist and turn in life so grand,
With clumsy feet, I make my stand.

So let's embrace this wild charade,
Where laughter looms and frowns are swayed.
In every stumble, a comic feat,
I dance through life, on wobbly feet.

The Fragility of Cheer

I wore my brightest smile today,
It sparkled like a fancy lamp.
But hidden in the laughter's sway,
My heart's a damp, cramped camp.

The clouds hold jokes, they spill them wide,
While I juggle thoughts like eggs.
With every slip, I run and hide,
The truth just waits, and begs.

My friends have maps to sunny shores,
But I'm stuck in a parking lot.
They laugh and dance while I adore,
The chaos that's drawing a plot.

Each giggle's just a clever mask,
Over brewing storms that tease.
I laugh to dodge every tough task,
Yet life's a trickster with ease.

Beneath the Sweetness

Underneath the sugar glaze,
Lurks a snack that's gone stale.
With every bite, I count the ways,
    I'm writing a funny tale.

The birthday cake is stacked so high,
    We cheer and sing out loud.
But crumbs fall down from dessert's sky,
    Leaving chuckles in the crowd.

A sippy cup spills in my lap,
    While I'm trying to look grand.
Each little mishap's a comic map,
    As I wipe with a shaky hand.

So here we are, a merry crew,
    With laughter in the mix.
While deep down, we all knew,
Life's a strange bag of tricks.

Threads of Sorrow

In the closet, hang my dreams,
Tangled up like knots of thread.
They whisper softly, or so it seems,
Tales I can't quite shed.

Each morning starts with color bright,
But soon fades into gray.
I wear a smile, oh what a sight,
As my worries dance and play.

I knit my hopes with swatches bold,
Each stitch a laugh, a tear.
Yet underneath, the truth is cold,
And that's the part I fear.

So if you see my yarn unwind,
Just know it's all for fun.
Life's a fabric, sweet and blind,
Stitched with laughter, on the run.

The Illusion of Ease

I stroll through life on roller skates,
With popcorn falling from my hands.
Each step I take, it resonates,
Like a clown at foolish stands.

The world spins round, a dizzy ride,
With every giggle, fate's a tease.
I dodge the bumps, with grace I slide,
Hiding my scuffs and unease.

A jester's cap upon my head,
I dance like no one's watching me.
But shadows whisper, fears are fed,
And that's the real comedy.

So let the laughter roll and ring,
As chaos finds its way to play.
With every tumble, there's a zing,
In this odd ballet, we sway.

Beneath the Gleam

Smiles plastered, teeth all bright,
Juggling chaos, what a sight.
Dancing under neon lights,
While the world unravels, it ignites.

Cupcakes melt in summer's heat,
Trying to run, but find my feet.
Sipping joy from paper cups,
With every slip, I raise my thumbs.

Witty banter, perfect jokes,
Crafted from a bag of hoax.
Behind the curtain, shadows loom,
Contorted laughter fills the room.

With painted eyes and pastel cheer,
My truth hides far, never near.
But oh, what fun to play this game,
In a world that's lost its flame.

Shattered Reflections

Mirrors crack with every grin,
Polished edges hide the sin.
I wear a mask of jester's glee,
While the truth just sips its tea.

Cookie crumbs on my lapel,
Laughing loudly, can't you tell?
Piles of laundry reach the sky,
But look at me, I can still fly!

Chasing dreams on skateboard wheels,
Crumbling under my spun reels.
Bubbles burst with every jest,
Yet I claim I'm at my best.

What's the scoop? Just a mirage,
Life is such a wild barrage.
In these shards, I find my way,
Half a laugh can save the day.

Veils of Contentment

Faux frolics and scripted cheer,
Butterflies stuck in a sphere.
Sipping tea from cracked porcelain,
Beneath it all, the rain won't wane.

With tangled thoughts and hopeful sighs,
I'll wave goodbye to cloudy skies.
Poised at the edge of the stage,
While thoughts of chaos write the page.

Feathered dreams in a bird cage,
Pretending life is all the rage.
Twirling tales with broken string,
Oh look, another perfect fling!

In gilded frames, I try to stand,
Smirking at the life unplanned.
But wrapped in silk, I can't unwind,
This playful jest is unconfined.

The Art of Pretending

Painting joy in every hue,
Waltzing with my inner zoo.
Sunshine smiles, electric rays,
Yet underneath, a tangled maze.

Feathers fly on puppet strings,
Bouncing with my borrowed wings.
Chasing laughter, lost in time,
But wait, is that a cynic's chime?

Frogs in suits, a wise old dance,
Cumerbunds in a wild prance.
Balderdash and silly jokes,
While the world sways, filled with hoax.

Behind the curtain, watches gleam,
A smirk reveals the hidden theme.
With every act, the heart concedes,
In jest, perhaps, we find our needs.

Navigating the Storm

Umbrellas dance like crazy birds,
While puddles plot our quick demise.
We skip and slip, oh haven't you heard?
The weather's mad, but so are the skies.

Rain boots squeak a silly tune,
As thunder claps with a wink and a grin.
We make our way beneath the moon,
Like sailors lost, but also kin.

A compass spins without a care,
Maps are drawn in crayon hues.
We'll get somewhere, I swear we'll share,
A laugh or two, life's best ruse!

So if the sky begins to cry,
We'll throw a party in this mess.
With wobbly steps, we'll splash and fly,
Oh, what a plot twist, I confess!

Glimmers of Gloom

A cloud of fluff, so gray yet bright,
Whispers of mischief and fun ahead.
Gloom invites us for a light fight,
While cheerful frowns are lovingly spread.

The sun sticks out its tongue at us,
With a wink and a hop in the air.
It's a circus, a funny little fuss,
We'll juggle our woes without a care.

A dance with shadows on the wall,
As rainbows peek through cracks of doubt.
In a world where silly is protocol,
Laughter's the key, no need to pout!

So grab a popcorn, watch the night,
As claps of joy burst with delight.
In this stage where we shine so bright,
Who knew gloom could feel so right?

A Canvas of Contradictions

Brush strokes of joy, splashes of gloom,
Colors collide in a big paint fight.
Doodles of chaos begin to bloom,
Masterpieces in the pale moonlight.

Life's an artist with a jiggly hand,
Mixing the sunny with shades of gray.
We giggle and snort, but we understand,
That smiles can spark in a puzzling way.

Swirls and twirls, oh, what a sight!
A canvas sprawling, oh so bizarre.
It's patchwork joy, the world's invite,
To dance through storms and reach for stars.

So let's paint our hearts without a plan,
In this funny art known as today.
We'll find the fun in the messy span,
Embrace the weird—hip hip hooray!

Broken Harmonies

A piano plays with a quirky sound,
Keys jump around, playing hide and seek.
Notes in a tangle, laughter abound,
A symphony of giggles at their peak.

The metronome ticks with an offbeat charm,
As melodies twist and tumble about.
In this cacophony, there's no alarm,
Just joyous chaos, full of clout.

We sing in voices both loud and small,
In harmony that's slightly askew.
Oh, how the ruckus doth enthrall,
When broken notes create something new!

So let's embrace this off-key spree,
For amidst the strum lies the heart's tune.
With every blunder, we're wild and free,
Dancing to laughs beneath the moon.

A Smile in Dissonance

With laughter loud and cheeks so bright,
I juggle woes, a comical sight.
A pratfall here, a slip or stumble,
Yet underneath, I quietly crumble.

My coffee's strong, my worries weak,
I laugh aloud, though not a peek.
Balancing joy like a circus act,
Inside a heart that's slightly cracked.

I tell tall tales of the day I've had,
While noisy thoughts dance mildly mad.
Jokes on the surface, chaos flows,
As smiles parade, my laughter grows.

In every pun and puny plight,
I hide the tears in shared delight.
So raise a glass to this charade,
Where happy faces cloak the fray.

Beneath the Surface of Tranquility

The garden blooms, a graceful guise,
Butterflies flit, the sun does rise.
Yet in the shade, a plant does sigh,
While crickets sing their lullaby.

The tea is steeped, the scones are sweet,
Yet crumbs of worry lie discreet.
I host a brunch of joy and cheer,
While turmoil winks, just out of ear.

A perfect cake with layers tall,
Each slice reveals a secret thrall.
I laugh at jokes, then pause to think,
As frothy smiles begin to sink.

So sip your cup, enjoy the show,
For underneath, the currents flow.
A mask of calm, a subtle jest,
In tranquil tides, I'm still a mess.

Echoes of Unraveled Threads

A sweater worn, with holes in seams,
I laugh and share my wildest dreams.
Each stitch a story, unraveling fast,
With tugging thoughts that hold me fast.

I find the humor in tangled yarn,
While knitting woes, I raise the alarm.
With every purl, I spin a tale,
Yet knots remain, I cannot bail.

In cozy corners, I sip my brew,
While socks of sorrow peek askew.
I'll knit a smile, in cheerful hues,
As mischief murmurs from worn-out shoes.

So pass the wool and let me weave,
These lightly woven tales deceive.
For laughter sounds a sweet refrain,
In clothing made of joy and pain.

The Art of Pretending

A dance of smiles, a skip, a prance,
In crowded rooms, I take my chance.
With feathered quips and cheery flair,
I hide the truth beneath the snare.

Like mixed-up tunes that don't align,
I scribble stories, craft the line.
With painted faces, our roles we play,
In the theater of the everyday.

A jest here and there, a wink, a nod,
While chaos bubbles like a fraud.
Behind the curtains, a wild show,
As I pretend to steal the glow.

Yet in the spotlight, I start to sway,
With laughter echoing, come what may.
So let's applaud this masquerade,
For life's a joke that we've all made.

Surface Tension

Smiles stretch wide like a rubber band,
But underneath, emotions can't withstand.
A wink and a nod, all seems so bright,
Yet whispers of chaos lurk out of sight.

Coffee spills on the cheerful floor,
As laughter echoes, but maybe it's sore.
A jester's mask hides the juggling pain,
While everyone dances, but few know the strain.

Plastic sunshine beams through the cracks,
While worries scatter like curious tax.
Punchlines wrapped up in a tangled plot,
Each laugh a cover for the truth we forgot.

So raise a toast with trembling hands,
To the charade that life demands.
A circus act where clowns are divine,
As we navigate mix-ups, all's not benign.

Echoes in a Hall of Mirrors

Reflections bounce with a hilarious charade,
All mirrors grinning, yet truth can't evade.
A punchline delivered with a mocking flair,
As we gather round, aware but unaware.

Behind every joke, a sigh is concealed,
While laughter erupts, the truth is revealed.
A giggle soars, then it trips on despair,
As echoes of smiles linger in midair.

Painted joy masks the unpolished dread,
In this hall of mirrors, we laugh as we bled.
Clowns juggling heartaches, a wild, lively spree,
But watch their faces; they're just like me.

So play the fool when the curtain drops,
For the audience cheers, yet the heart never stops.
We dance and we jest, under the spotlight's glow,
In the carnival of life, the real show is low.

A Beautiful Deceit

Balloons painted bright, hiding a draught,
With confetti falling, each heart's left caught.
We toast to the funny, while troubles reside,
In a world full of laughter, the truth must abide.

Jokes crack like eggs, messy and fun,
Underlying yolks that we dare not shun.
A comedy sketch where the punchline's amiss,
While the audience claps, it's a hit or a miss.

Frivolous giggles can't mask the dread,
In a banquet of smiles, who's stuffing their bread?
The cake slice may look sweet, but oh, take care,
A hint of despair lingers in the air.

So we dance on the edge of humor and pain,
Each joke a lifebuoy, but none will remain.
In this beautiful deceit, we twirl and we spin,
As laughter's disguise wraps the chaos within.

The Hidden Cradle of Turmoil

Underneath the jester's clownish grin,
Lies a stormy tempest brewing within.
We spin tales of joy while shadows encroach,
In the hidden cradle where secrets broach.

Juggling fears like a playful ruse,
While hoping the truth won't hit us with blues.
A merry parade, but the floats are askew,
As laughter erupts, the tears slip on through.

Ribbons and sparkles covering the scars,
In this comedy club, we toast to our wars.
With every punchline, a heart softly trembles,
For under the surface, our misery resembles.

So raise up a glass to the laughter we chase,
While chaos hums softly, a waltz in the space.
As we all play the part of the humorously fine,
In the hidden cradle where turmoil'll align.

Shadows of Contentment

A sunny grin hides a frown,
Like a clown wearing a crown.
With laughter that can sometimes crack,
While troubles stack up in a pack.

Chasing joy like a wayward breeze,
Dodging worries like buzzing bees.
The pie's a pie while it's still raw,
Waiting for life to drop the jaw.

Sipping tea with one eye closed,
Telling tales that no one knows.
A wiggle and a jiggle here,
Hiding chaos, full of cheer.

But if you peek behind the light,
You'll find the shadows, not so bright.
Dancing with a twisted grin,
In a world of chaos, I still spin.

Behind the Smiles

In the mirror, a grin so wide,
Hiding the stumbles I confide.
Each chuckle a well-timed act,
Joyful snap, but that's a fact.

Cracking jokes on a wobbly stage,
While the script is filled with rage.
The punchline hits, the chuckles flow,
Still wondering how low I can go.

Wit and whimsy cloak the mess,
Laughing loudly, just to impress.
But between the snaps and silly games,
Are echoes of forgotten names.

So here we stand, in this charade,
With merry masks, we dance, we parade.
Yet once the curtain takes its fall,
What's left is a silence, not a call.

The Mask I Wear

A jester's hat upon my head,
With painted smiles, I tread ahead.
Inside me churns a different tale,
With vivid dreams that often pale.

The mask I wear, so bright and bold,
Hides the story yet untold.
A little grin and a silly twirl,
While the inner chaos starts to swirl.

Jokes and giggles, a fine façade,
Yet underneath lies my charade.
Tickling ribs with a wink and nudge,
While deeper woes refuse to budge.

So I dance on this precarious line,
Beneath the sparkle, there's no sign.
Yet when night falls and here I dwell,
It's a secret I know all too well.

Whispers of Dissonance

A tune that's stuck, some offbeat notes,
With laughter laced in tangled quotes.
The sunlight sings, but clouds are near,
A colorful mess, yet we persevere.

Conversations in a jumbled style,
Finding giggles in every mile.
The punchline lands but feels askew,
Dissonance in what we pursue.

I chuckle loud to drown the sigh,
Yet the echo feels a little shy.
Swinging high on the mood's pendulum,
Between silly fun and a heavy drum.

Each chuckle veils a worry's trace,
In jest, I find a hiding place.
With every laugh, a whispered truth,
A dance of joy that conceals our youth.

The Calm Within the Chaos

In a whirlwind of socks and snacks,
I stand here with my coffee attacks.
Bubbles burst and dishes dance,
Yet somehow, it feels like a chance.

Laughter hides beneath each sigh,
As the ceiling fan begins to fly.
The dog wears a hat, quite the sight,
In this circus, chaos feels just right.

My plants look shocked from their pots,
Who knew they'd witness such lots?
But here I sip, the world amiss,
Counting each imperfection with bliss.

Let's toast to the mess, the joyful wreck,
To the clueless cat on my tech deck.
For in this tornado, I do embrace,
Simple smiles in a frantic race.

The Mirage of Contentment

It's a facade of a perfect scene,
With laundry hampers fit for a queen.
I smile wide, my hair in a knot,
Pretending I've got everything thought.

My dinner's a remake of last week's prank,
But with herbs for flair, I'll hold the tank.
Forks and spoons in perfect disarray,
I'll claim it's a buffet, come what may.

The remote's lost, but don't you fret,
I'll find it 'neath that old, dusty pet.
While crumbs like confetti cover my path,
I'll dance with joy in the aftermath.

So raise your glass, fellow fools,
To the grand illusion that life just cools.
For amid the quirks and tangled threads,
We find our laughter instead of dreads.

Drowning in Calm Waters

In a sea of emails and stray old socks,
I float like a boat with glittery docks.
The calm is a mask that nearly fools,
While the toaster duel brews homemade ghouls.

I paddle through breakfast with jelly and bread,
As the cat forms a bed like a true demo lead.
Navigating tides of misfit toys,
Crafting calm amidst a raucous noise.

The couch is a throne with snacks piled high,
Yet under the cushions, old mysteries lie.
I sip my drink while chaos declares,
That a hall of odd socks is no cause for fears.

So here's to the waves that rock our little boat,
As I balance my worries on this lovely moat.
For in this adventure of style and strife,
I'll spin my helical laughter through life.

The Beauty of the Mask

With painted smiles and grins so wide,
I take the stage, and in I glide.
Beneath the sparkle, there's all that's wrong,
But the show must go on; can't break the song.

I juggle excuses like a pro in a play,
While the world spins madly, come what may.
A tap dance of folly throughout the day,
To keep the uncertain moments at bay.

I laugh at the past, though it's often a fright,
With glitter in hand, I'll dance through the night.
For life's a performance with scenes that aren't keen,
But watch as I twirl in this dreamlike routine.

So cheer for the act, for every misstep,
For the joy in the blur, I'm just taking a rep.
In a theater made from our chaos and space,
I'll wear my mask proudly, with style and grace.

Chasing Illusive Horizons

On the path of happy smiles,
My socks have danced for miles.
Yet the sun's playing hide and seek,
While my shoes let out a squeak.

Clouds pout where sunshine should be,
Like my dreams, they flee from me.
With each step, a laugh escapes,
It's a joy ride of silly shapes.

The grass whispers, 'All is well',
Yet my donut had a swell.
With every giggle, life unfolds,
Fancied tales that fun retolds.

Chasing mirages in the breeze,
Gremlins juggling all my keys.
While smiles reign, my woes entwine,
And still, we dance—oh, it's just fine!

The Deceptive Stillness

Sitting in my cozy chair,
Reality's a tasty fare.
The cat's plotting world domination,
While I sip my concoction of speculation.

The clock ticks at a playful pace,
Tickling my sanity, it's a race.
But things are quiet, barely a peep,
Except for dreams that make me leap.

I wore a smile, thought I'd shine,
Yet missed the train—oh, what a sign!
PJs say I'm winning life,
But laundry's lurking, causing strife.

The stillness mocks with a wink,
As I ponder the cosmic kink.
But hey, my cake's a double slice,
And moments like these sure are nice!

Illusions of Contentment

Twirling in my happiness bliss,
With a cake or two I won't miss.
The world spins with glitter and flair,
Though my heart's tangled in despair.

I giggle at the absurd parade,
As socks and shoes begin to trade.
In a whirl of streamers, life doth play,
While I roller skate through disarray.

Smiling all the way to the beach,
Holding a jester's outstretched reach.
The sun beams like it knows the score,
Yet I've misplaced my keys once more.

Contentment's a mask I wear so bright,
While my worries take flight at night.
But laughter's the key, my secret bright,
In this circus of delightful fright.

Hues of Unrest

Painting dreams in colors bold,
But the sky can't take the mold.
With each stroke, the chaos swirls,
As my optimism unravels and twirls.

Life's a canvas, a jolly ruse,
Yet all I find are mismatched shoes.
The colors clash, a wild spree,
With laughter ringing out like glee.

While rainbows fade into the gray,
I sell my calm for a joke to play.
With every brush, I swoosh and dive,
Making sure that chaos thrives.

In hues of unrest, I find my way,
With splashes and giggles here to stay.
For amid the mess, we fashion a rhyme,
In the weirdest of places, we find our prime.

The Weight of a Smile

A grin so wide, it hurts my cheeks,
But underneath, a storm still peaks.
Innocent eyes, a playful guise,
As the truth secretly sneaks.

Juggling joy, while frowning inside,
A comedy show where I must hide.
Clown shoes too big, tripping in style,
Another act of laughable pride.

With every chuckle, we bury our woes,
Beneath the humor, a river flows.
For in this circus, we all must play,
Even when sunshine too often slows.

So I wear my mask, and dance about,
In this grand show, let's laugh and shout.
For life's a jest, a comic relief,
With hidden stories we never doubt.

A Tapestry of Tension

We weave our laughs with threads of doubt,
In the fabric of life, we twist and shout.
A needle pricks, we joke around,
While all the seams are coming unbound.

Dancing on edge, where humor's a plight,
Comedic timing, a delicate flight.
We stitch our smiles with a sigh or two,
Ripping the seams of what's really true.

With threads of joy stitched tight to despair,
We patch it up like we just don't care.
A tapestry bright, yet frayed at the ends,
Tales of laughter, and all that depends.

Each knot we tie hides a little fright,
In this quilt of quips, we pretend it's right.
For life may unravel, but humor's our thread,
We'll laugh through the chaos, not tears but instead.

When Laughter Masks Pain

A joyful outburst, but not so sincere,
Hiding the whispers of something unclear.
Behind every punchline, a heart-ache beats,
Under the chuckles, a quiet retreat.

We swap our sorrows for jokes that we share,
In this circus of pain, we all must prepare.
For every giggle hides a cloudy thought,
Each laugh's a lesson in the battles we've fought.

So bring out the clown, let him wear my face,
While inside, I'm lost in an infinite space.
Yet, there's warmth in the chaos, a glimmer of fun,
As laughter rings bright, like rays from the sun.

In this masquerade ball, we twirl and we spin,
Both the jesters and kings wear a mask of chagrin.
For under the humor, we're all just the same,
Searching for solace, forgetting the blame.

Dancing on the Edge

On the tightrope of joy, I sway and I grin,
Balancing woes on the edge of a pin.
The audience chuckles, enthralled by my dance,
While I juggle my thoughts like they stand a chance.

With no safety net, I pirouette fast,
Winking at moments where shadows are cast.
Each slip just a quip, as I flirt with the fall,
Ignoring the fact that I'm teetering tall.

A split-seconds laugh, and the air feels so light,
I'm spinning tales 'til they vanish from sight.
Yet hidden beneath this tightrope's delight,
Are whispers of worries that flicker at night.

So I dance on the edge, a fool in disguise,
With laughter my armor, as truth softly lies.
For the stage is set, and I'm part of the show,
In this waltz of absurdity, I'll steal the glow.

Shadows of Discontent

In the corner, the laundry piles high,
Socks on a mission, they wave goodbye.
Dishes are talking, they've got some dirt,
But I'm just here, in my cozy survey.

Coffee cup tumbles, a dance on the floor,
Caffeine spills like my promises, more and more.
Plants pretend to thrive, they've got a charade,
While I question decisions I've so proudly made.

The cat's plotting world domination, you see,
As I chuckle and sip, it's all just a spree.
Life's a circus, that's no surprise,
With a ringmaster giggling behind weary eyes.

Whispers of chaos float through the air,
Like balloons I released, too light to care.
But here I sit, with popcorn in hand,
Laughing at shadows that won't understand.

Silent Cries

Under the desk, my lunch has grown legs,
Pasta rebellion, it's doing the pegs.
I laugh at the chaos all around me,
While my coffee cup winks, oh so cheeky.

Another deadline, like a game of tag,
While my to-do list steals my old swag.
The printer is wheezing, a true loud punk,
As the clock ticks in rhythm, I'm feeling the funk.

A sneeze disrupts the office's hush,
And suddenly silence breaks into a rush.
But I'm tucked in my bubble, too busy to heed,
The drama unfolding while I'm quite freed.

A dance of the papers, a whirlwind so bright,
I giggle alone in the fluorescent light.
In the midst of the storm, I keep my own beat,
While time plays hopscotch, oh what a feat!

A Symphony of Discord

Life is a band where instruments clash,
The trumpet, the tuba, it's quite a splash.
In the corner, the clarinet sighs,
As the piano throws notes, swirling in lies.

The drummer insists it's a jazzy affair,
While the violin sings like it doesn't care.
I tap to the rhythm, my feet in a whirl,
As chaos plays on, like a tempestuous girl.

A concert of mishaps, I giggle and grin,
Juggling my sanity, the show must begin.
Bowed strings break down, while brass hits the high,
And I'm here just wondering, "Why did I try?"

But amidst all the noise, I find my own tune,
With laughter as my guide, I sway to the boon.
For in this orchestra, I shall compose,
A melody joyful, while discord still grows.

Mismatched Melodies

Socks and shoes, they never agree,
One's off to the left, the other's a flea.
My hair's got its own style, in full disarray,
As I wander through life, in a silly ballet.

The toaster is humming a tune of its own,
While I misplace my keys, are they on loan?
Emails are piling, I'm lost in the haze,
While I sing my own song through this chaotic maze.

The fridge is a symphony of forgotten cheese,
As I dance with the ghosts of unwashed peas.
Each day is a different off-key serenade,
As I laugh through the mess that I've bravely made.

A cat in the window, a chorus so bright,
As I juggle my worries, it feels so right.
Life's an orchestrated, mismatched display,
And I'll waltz through this carnival, come what may.

Shadows in the Sun

With a smile that's painted bright,
I juggle my woes, what a sight!
Sunshine shines, but I trip and fall,
Yet on I skip, pretending it's all.

The ice cream melts quicker than plans,
As I dance with my invisible fans.
Laughter bubbles, but oh dear me,
The punchline's stuck in a quagmire spree.

In the light, I cast my own shade,
Where jokes are good, but truth's delayed.
Behind the facade, the laughter might fade,
Still I march on, a masquerade.

Clouds float by, their secrets unspun,
While I trip over my own pun.
Cartwheeling through the day's silly strife,
Blindly I sway, it's a comical life.

The Weight of Pretence

Wearing smiles like a tailored suit,
I stomp through life, mute toot to toot.
Beneath my jokes, a circus clown,
But oh, this laughter's wearing me down.

Each witticism, a weight on my chest,
Like a bad joke that never finds rest.
I balance my woes on an outstretched hand,
While the universe giggles at my grand stand.

Dancing through drama, I misstep and sway,
Pretend it's a ball when it's just a ballet.
With each quip, the truth slips away,
Yet here I am, in this comedic play.

So I chuckle and roll with each stumble,
In the realm of humor, heartbeats fumble.
With every laugh, I wear my disguise,
A jester in life's oversized guise.

Crutches of Comfort

On my crutches made of cotton candy,
I stroll through chaos, a bit uncanny.
With sprinkles of hope on a doughnut treat,
I bounce through the mess, all dressed up neat.

Life's a circus, and I'm in the show,
While juggling worries that never let go.
A clown shoe trip, but I just can't fall,
For laughter's the key to my grand hall.

Twirling on stilts of marshmallow dreams,
I pirouette around impossible schemes.
With each misstep, my audience roars,
As I waltz through life and lock all the doors.

So here I stand, a beacon of jest,
With sugar-coated humor, I feel so blessed.
In the carnival of chaos, let's just unwind,
Where the cracks of reality are brightly designed.

A Portrait of Paradox

Here's a picture, bright and surreal,
Framed with laughter, but what's the deal?
The canvas laughs while shadows conspire,
Painting a world where joys don't tire.

With a wink and a nudge, I tiptoe around,
While the ground opens wide, making no sound.
In a gallery filled with giggles and weeps,
Art imitates life in chaotic heaps.

I juggle the colors of joy and despair,
As the brush strokes whisper secrets rare.
Each layer of paint hides tales yet untold,
In the museum of life, where smiles grow old.

So behold, this odd tapestry spun,
Where every thread fights to come undone.
In the laughter, the sadness finds rhyme,
And we keep on laughing, one verse at a time.

Serene in the Chaos

My socks don't match, it's all a spree,
A dance of chaos, just look at me!
The coffee spills and the cat goes wild,
Yet in this mess, I'm still a child.

With papers scattered, all in disgrace,
I wear my smile like a cozy face.
The world spins on, a topsy-turvy ride,
I clutch my sanity where fears reside.

Beneath the laughter, bubbles of cheer,
Lie silly worries that refuse to clear.
Yet here I stand, with arms spread wide,
A jester in the court, enjoying the tide.

So let the chaos spin, let it twirl,
In this silly dance, I still can whirl.
With quirky glee, I face the strife,
In my own circus, I clown my life.

The Hidden Struggles

Behind my grin lies a circus show,
Where clowns juggle woe with a dash of glow.
I'd join the tightrope, but oh, the fear,
Yet laughter's just a cry in disguise here.

Eating cookies to drown all the doubt,
While pretending I'm fine, just figuring it out.
A tiptoed dance on a lined-up seam,
As I stitch together this wobbly dream.

The world keeps spinning as I take a breath,
Haunted by shadows, but I'll cheat death.
With snickers and giggles, I'll carry on,
In my messy play, I am never gone.

With my heart on a pogo stick, bouncing high,
I'm winking at troubles like they don't apply.
In my hidden struggles, I find my way,
Painting a smile on a rainy day.

Beneath Delicate Layers

My skin is fragile, like worn-out lace,
Yet here I am, wearing a funny face.
Beneath the layers, I'm soft like pie,
But life's a pie fight, I aim for the sky.

With hats of laughter, I cover my plight,
While juggling dreams in the pale moonlight.
Behind closed doors, the world might hear,
A symphony played on my hidden fear.

With grand illusions of coffee and cheer,
I stand like a trophy, bright and sincere.
Yet in the shadows, I practice my lines,
For the show's not over till the punchline shines.

So pass me the confetti; let laughter ignite,
I'll dance through the mess and twirl through the night.
In delicate layers, I embrace the haze,
Finding delight in this wobbly maze.

The Quiet Battle

In the battle of whispers where silence reigns,
I wear my armor made of paper chains.
Stepping lightly on the edge of grace,
While the world's a riot in this calm space.

With my trusty sidekick, a slice of cake,
I wage my war—oh, for goodness' sake!
The laughter erupts from the cracks of time,
A muffled giggle, a joke without rhyme.

In corners of chaos, I twirl and I spin,
Holding up signs that say, "Let's dive in!"
And oh, the fun of this quiet charade,
Where dreams and worries so comfortably braid.

With a wink to the stars that light up the night,
The quiet battle is a magical sight.
Amidst the mayhem, I find my smile,
In the dance of the absurd, I'll stay for a while.

Unraveling Threads

Spilled coffee stains on my shirt,
A dog stole my lunch, oh what a flirt.
Chaos reigns in the kitchen space,
I find a lost sock, what a funny case.

My cat greets me with a knowing stare,
As I trip on my hopes like a friendly bear.
Juggling tasks like clowns at a show,
But it's all under control, or so I haphazardly know.

The laundry's a mountain, the dishes a sea,
Guess the chaos is somehow a part of me.
I wear a smile that's ready to crack,
Like a piñata filled with nonsense, ready to whack.

Yet in this mess, joy finds its place,
Like a long-lost friend, wearing a silly face.
So here's to the chaos, let it reign free,
With laughter and quirks, it's a sight to see.

The Comfort of Chaos

Waking up late, the alarm's gone wrong,
Burnt toast serenades with a crispy song.
Shoes on the wrong feet, I walk like a fool,
While the morning greets me with its usual duel.

The cat's on my laptop, living her dreams,
While I sip my coffee, it's bursting at the seams.
Emails await with their urgent little cries,
But my pajama pants seem the best disguise.

The plants on my shelf are not feeling fine,
They look at me sideways, a judgmental line.
Yet I smile wide, despite the fray,
Like a clown in a circus, come what may.

Living in chaos feels oddly right,
With each little blunder, I soar to new height.
So here's to the mess, my life's shiny crown,
Where laughter's the glue that won't let me down.

Echoes of Denial

I tell myself daily, 'Today's gonna shine,'
But the toaster just laughed, burned toast, oh divine.
In the mirror, I wear a perplexed grin,
Like I planned this disaster, where do I begin?

My plants keep on thriving in neglected rows,
They're thriving on chaos, who really knows?
Dust bunnies dance like they own the floor,
And yet I insist, 'I couldn't care more!'

My kids run wild with a gleeful shout,
While I ponder if sanity's just a thought out.
Emails pile high, but there's cake to be made,
I'll get to it later, I've got games to play.

In this circus of mess, I manage to thrive,
With laughter as my compass, I'm truly alive.
Let chaos unfurl, let it wrap me tight,
For in this wild storm, I'll dance in delight.

Illusions of Joy

With a grin on my face, I greet the day bright,
But my shoes have decided to start a small fight.
The dryer hums tunes of mismatched socks,
And my cereal's swimming like nautical clocks.

I ran out of milk, surely that's fate,
So I concoct a smoothie that tastes like a plate.
But my blender protests with a choppy delight,
As it spews out my breakfast, oh what a sight!

Kids in the background play tag with my brain,
While I sip on some coffee that once was plain.
The chaos spins 'round like a carnival ride,
But hey, let's embrace this wild, silly tide.

For joy wears a hat made of mismatched threads,
And laughter's the pillow on which chaos treads.
So here's to the circus that life tends to be,
Where the punchline comes first, and I'm giggling with glee!

The Quiet Disarray

My socks don't match, nor do my shoes,
The coffee's cold, I've got the blues.
Yet here I sit with a crooked smile,
Waiting for chaos to settle a while.

The cat's on the table, the dog on the chair,
Spaghetti's splattered—who says I care?
The clock is ticking, but I'm in no rush,
Life's a wild ride, and I'm in a hush.

Juggling my worries like a circus clown,
While every little thing keeps tumbling down.
I laugh at the mess, what more can I do?
Embracing the chaos in my own view.

So let the world spin with its quirky dance,
I'll wear my mismatches, give joy a chance.
In this lovely disarray, I'm feeling so free,
Laughing at life, oh dear, look at me!

Smiling Through the Pain

Woke up this morning with a coffee spill,
Tripped on my laces but I've got the will.
With toothpaste on my shirt and my hair like a bird,
I'm grinning wide, not caring, absurd.

Life's full of bumps like a cheesy ride,
But I'm a jokester with hope as my guide.
Naps are a treasure, I snooze and I dream,
While laughter keeps weaving my delicate seam.

With a skip and a hop, I conquer my fears,
Dancing through puddles while holding back tears.
Boss mode is on, with my quirks out to play,
"Oh, don't mind the chaos!" is my proud display.

I wear all my battles like a comic book flair,
Turning every mishap into a laugh-filled affair.
So if you see me, just shake your head,
I'll be the one smiling, all dressed up in red!

Warped Reflections

Look in the mirror, what do I see?
A funny-faced stranger just winking at me.
With hair standing tall like a cactus in bloom,
I giggle and shudder, embrace the wild room.

Reflections are twisted, oh, what a sight!
Waving hello to my jester at night.
A smile in the glass and a cackle in tow,
As I dance through the awkward and let my joy flow.

Juggling my fears like a clown on a stage,
Each step a skit, oh, the laughter's the gauge!
With a fumble and tumble, I leap and I spin,
In this circus of life, let the fun times begin!

So here's to the quirks, the silly mistakes,
I'll laugh at the chaos, embrace what it takes.
My reflection's a story, a riddle, a play,
Where humor is wisdom, come join, if you may!

The Veil of Normal

Living like normal, or so I pretend,
But my sanity's humming, will it ever mend?
A sock on my hand like a glove in disguise,
   Making a mockery of all of life's lies.

I wave at the traffic from my kitchen chair,
While my cake's in the oven, turning into despair.
Yet I summon my giggles as things go awry,
   Grin when the pizza's a pastry pie!

With a denim jacket over polka dots bright,
I strut down the sidewalk, a ridiculous sight.
Each step's a reminder that normal's a game,
And I'm just the player—not wanting the fame.

So let the world whirl in its glossy façade,
I'll keep on the fun, and nod with a nod.
For behind all the laughter, my heart finds its rhyme,
In a dance made of jest, in the realm of time.

Chasing Shadows of Bliss

In the park, where laughter rings,
I wear my smile, like feath'ry wings.
Yet a squirrel steals my sandwich slice,
Guess my happiness comes with a price.

With a grin that's slightly askew,
I dance like no one sees me, it's true.
But I trip on the grass, oh what a view,
Laughing at life, and its funny due.

Chasing shadows as the sun starts to sink,
I sip my coffee, but it's more like ink.
A jester at heart, in a jester's disguise,
Yet here come the clowns with no pies to surprise.

So here's to the circus that's really my day,
With punchlines hidden in pots of clay.
When life hands me lemons, I start a parade,
With confetti and giggles, I won't be dismayed.

Between the Lines

I'm reading a book, it's a thrilling tale,
But I can't understand why my ship's gone stale.
The hero's fine, with brave sword and shield,
While I'm stuck here with cereal unrevealed.

The pages turn, but my life's on pause,
There's dust on my dreams, I'm starting to snooze.
With a wink and a nod, the plot thickens fast,
Yet my coffee's cold, and my hopes are amassed.

Plot twists abound in the literary scene,
While I'm over here, stuck in limbo routine.
"Just one more chapter," I earnestly plead,
But my fridge is empty, I really must feed.

Between the lines, I search for a cue,
But my snacks are gone, and my patience too.
So I'll scribble a note, "Next time, bring snacks,"
And laugh at the chaos, with all its cracks.

The Cost of Composure

In a suit that's tailored and shoes that shine,
I juggle my work, looking just so divine.
But beneath this surface, I'm losing my cool,
Like a kid with a secret in a room full of fools.

My coffee's on schedule, my tie's too tight,
As I ponder whether to take flight at night.
With spreadsheets and meetings, my joys are all hidden,
While I mime to the copier, my laughter forbidden.

The pressure mounts, like a cake made of bricks,
Wondering when life became one of its tricks.
I perfect my grin, it's a marvelous show,
But under the surface, I'm ready to go.

The boss cracks a joke, it's met with a sigh,
As I pledge my allegiance to the pie in the sky.
So I smile and nod, as my brain starts to rust,
Laughing at the mayhem, it's a feel-good must.

The Mirror's Lie

There's a reflection, oh what a sight,
It says I'm radiant, just full of delight.
But inside I'm battling a phantom of dread,
In pajamas so comfy, I'd rather be fed.

With eyes bright as stars, or so the mirror insists,
Yet my breakfast is half-baked, I've learned to resist.
I smile at my hair, it's as wild as a spree,
Now where's that fairy godmother, plea-hee!

It shows me a hero, a fearless brave knight,
Though I'm cloaked in my blanket, just ready to write.
I've jotted some doodles, they look like a mess,
But they capture the chaos—my gentle distress.

The mirror keeps grinning, it knows all my tricks,
As I ponder if "today" can include a quick fix.
So I tip my hat to that wild-eyed disguise,
For laughter and fluffies are surely my prize.

In the Shade of Sadness

Under a tree, I fake a grin,
Spilled lemonade, my chaos within.
The birds don't listen, they just sing,
While I juggle woes like a clown in spring.

Ice cream cones melt in the sun,
I trip on shadows, oh what fun!
With every hiccup, I laugh aloud,
Dancing with clouds, wrapped in a shroud.

Why does the toaster always burn?
My courage crumbles, what's the turn?
I wear mismatched socks as my badge,
In my circus of life, I'm the raggamuffin sage.

Sipping my troubles in a teacup,
Oh, my imaginary friend just won't shut up!
In this comedy, I'm the punchline,
Winking at fate, sipping on sunshine.

The Dissonant Dance

Tap shoes on the floor, a clumsy beat,
Twisting and turning on shaky feet.
My partner's a ghost of missed romance,
We twirl together in a quirky dance.

In a waltz with worries, I take the lead,
Stumbling and mumbling, oh yes indeed!
The music's a mess, the rhythm's gone,
Yet here I am, dancing till dawn.

With juggling pins of my daily grind,
I flail through life, never defined.
A flip, a twirl, the spotlight's a tease,
Laughing at chaos, oh, what a breeze!

The audience snickers, I bow with flair,
Not quite together, but I don't care.
In this cacophony, I find my way,
Each misstep a story, come dance and play!

An Architect of Anxiety

I draw blueprints with shaky hands,
Sketching my hope on shifting sands.
With bricks of doubt and windows of fear,
I build a castle, then disappear.

Plans in a drawer, like lost love notes,
My architect dreams float on tiny boats.
Stumbling through hallways of what-ifs,
Each corner a whisper, dodging the rifts.

In the attic of worries, I hide my crown,
Constructing scenarios wearing a frown.
A spire of laughter peeks through the gloom,
As I plan for a feast in my cluttered room.

Galas of panic, the guest list is grand,
With party hats made from the world's demand.
I unscrew the hinges on hope's fragile door,
To let laughter in, who could ask for more?

Threads of Uncertainty

With yarn of worries, I knit my day,
Each stitch a question, a wobbly sway.
My scarf gets longer, a patchwork of dread,
Yet somehow I wear it, a hat on my head.

Purls of confusion, knit one, slip two,
Turning gray clouds into bright shades of blue.
A tangled mess of hopes tied in knots,
Yet I weave on, amidst all the plots.

Fabrics of laughter hide the seams,
In a tapestry woven with hopeful dreams.
I dance with the threads that fray and break,
Creating a masterpiece, my heart's warm ache.

So here I sit, stitching up strife,
Crafting a quilt of this silly life.
Each thread a giggle, a joyful spin,
In this fabric of chaos, I'm ready to win!

Behind Closed Doors

In the kitchen, a dance ensues,
Spaghetti flour on the dog's shoes.
The cat stares, judging with flair,
While I pretend I don't care.

My plants all whisper, 'We need some sun,'
I nod along, but it's all in fun.
The dishes pile high, like my dreams,
Yet laughter echoes, or so it seems.

Outside, the world spins, a chaotic show,
Inside, I juggle my own little foe.
Capable of grace, I promise a meal,
Just pray that the smoke alarm doesn't squeal.

Behind the doors, chaos is bliss,
In this circus of joy, nothing's amiss.
Crazy is normal, or so it's declared,
Just keep on dancing, pretend we don't care.

A Quiet Tumult

The coffee pot brews with a moan,
I sigh, wishing for a throne.
The toast is burnt, but it's hard to see,
When everything's moving, not just me.

The dog is howling in perfect pitch,
While my hopes of calm go down the ditch.
I sip my cup, just need a break,
As the cat steals my bagel with glee, for heaven's sake.

The clock's ticking louder than the news,
Tick-tock chaos, life's old ruse.
I smile, pretending I'm all put together,
While navigating through this funny weather.

Among the stillness, a ruckus prevails,
I'm silently screaming while humor entails.
In the quiet tumult, absurdity reigns,
Laughing at life's little, messy gains.

Smiles in the Ruins

Amidst the spilled milk and stack of clothes,
A bubble of laughter, it gently grows.
The kids are wild, like leaves in a storm,
Yet smiles bloom in this chaotic norm.

Dead plants nod, yes, they too feel grand,
Waving their brown leaves in perfect demand.
The laundry awaits with an ever-growing pile,
Yet the giggles are worth every single mile.

Post-it notes plastered, reminders galore,
To "breathe" and "smile," but is there more?
The world's a joke wrapped in confetti,
We're just the punchline, all feeling ready.

In this patchwork of wreckage, joy finds a way,
Worn-out shoes still dance through the fray.
With laughter as glue, we'll patch up the seams,
Smiles in the ruins, we're living the dreams.

The Burden of Normalcy

On Tuesday's visit, I dust off the plan,
To be a grown-up, here's how it ran.
Grocery lists and a clean kitchen fate,
Clothes on the floor like a family crate.

I wear my smile, but it's a tad askew,
Like puzzle pieces that barely stick too.
While the neighbors chatter about all things right,
I bubble with laughter, preparing for flight.

The vacuum protests like a grumpy old man,
Stepping around dust bunnies, I ramble and scan.
I promise next week I'll get it all right,
But here comes the cat, diving past in mid-flight.

In this burden of normalcy, I find my way,
Every little flaw leads to a brighter day.
So cheers to chaos, I'll wear it like pride,
A jester's crown, with laughter as my guide.